# Achieving Authentic Wealth
Building Prosperity for the Right Reasons

## Workbook

Achieving Authentic Wealth Workbook
Published by Guy Thing Press
P.O. Box 827
Roanoke, TX 76262

This book or parts thereof may not be reproduced in any form, stored in a retrieval system, or transmitted in any form by any means - electronic, mechanical, photocopy, recording, or otherwise - without prior written permission of the publisher, except as provided by United States of America copyright law.

Guy Thing Press books may be purchased in bulk for educational, business, fund-raising, or sales promotional use. For more information, please contact Guy Thing Press.

Please visit us at www.guythingpress.com

Copyright © 2008 by Guy Thing Press
All Rights Reserved

*Printed in the United States of America*

ISBN-13: 978-0-9818337-6-7
ISBN-10: 0-9818337-6-4

Scripture taken from the New King James Version. Copyright © 1982 by Thomas Nelson, Inc. Used by permission. All rights reserved.

# Contents

Preparing for Wealth . . . . . . . . . . . . . . . . . . . . . . . . . . . . . . . . . . . . . . . 1

Multiplying Money into Wealth . . . . . . . . . . . . . . . . . . . . . . . . . . . . . 5

How to Lose Your Wealth . . . . . . . . . . . . . . . . . . . . . . . . . . . . . . . . . 11

Creating Generational Wealth . . . . . . . . . . . . . . . . . . . . . . . . . . . . . 17

How to Maintain the Wealth and Blessing of God . . . . . . . . . . . . . . 23

The Real Purpose of Wealth . . . . . . . . . . . . . . . . . . . . . . . . . . . . . . . 29

Blessing or Curse; It's Your Choice . . . . . . . . . . . . . . . . . . . . . . . . . 35

Consider Abraham . . . . . . . . . . . . . . . . . . . . . . . . . . . . . . . . . . . . . 41

Leave… And Go to the Land I Will Show You . . . . . . . . . . . . . . . . 47

Leave Ur . . . . . . . . . . . . . . . . . . . . . . . . . . . . . . . . . . . . . . . . . . . . . 53

They Came to Haran . . . . . . . . . . . . . . . . . . . . . . . . . . . . . . . . . . . 57

He Set Out from Haran . . . . . . . . . . . . . . . . . . . . . . . . . . . . . . . . . 61

He Went On Toward the Hills . . . . . . . . . . . . . . . . . . . . . . . . . . . . 67

Set Out and Continue . . . . . . . . . . . . . . . . . . . . . . . . . . . . . . . . . . 73

Went Down to Egypt . . . . . . . . . . . . . . . . . . . . . . . . . . . . . . . . . . . 79

He Went From Place to Place . . . . . . . . . . . . . . . . . . . . . . . . . . . . . 85

He Came to Bethel . . . . . . . . . . . . . . . . . . . . . . . . . . . . . . . . . . . . . 91

Lot Was Moving About With Abram . . . . . . . . . . . . . . . . . . . . . . . 97

The Lord Said to Abram . . . . . . . . . . . . . . . . . . . . . . . . . . . . . . . . 101

The Purpose of Prosperity . . . . . . . . . . . . . . . . . . . . . . . . . . . . . . 105

# Chapter 1
Preparing for Wealth

# Achieving Authentic Wealth

1. In order to enter into a place you have never been, you must _____ _____.

2. What is the purpose of the "qualifying time" the author speaks of?
   _____
   _____
   _____

3. Our _____ is of little concern to God, but our _____ is.

4. What did Einstein consider to be "insanity"?
   _____
   _____
   _____

5. Why do you have to change?
   _____
   _____

6. Your life is no longer your own. You must decide that following the ways and the _____ _____ takes precedence over everything else in your life.

7. What is the sowing/reaping principle of God and what is it meant for?
   _____
   _____
   _____

# Chapter 1
## Preparing for Wealth

8. What does the word "need" mean and how does God provide for it?

_____
_____
_____

9. What can you expect if you are currently spending according to the plans of God?

_____
_____
_____

10. What misleading idea have we believed regarding the ability to get money?

_____
_____

11. How many of the tribes in Israel were NOT of the priesthood? What was their focus supposed to be?

_____
_____
_____

12. What is change?

_____
_____

13. God never demands or expects prosperity at the expense of _____.

14. What priorities should a Christian have in their life?

# Chapter 1
# Preparing for Wealth

# Chapter 1
# Preparing for Wealth

# Key Point Review

1. What can you do to begin preparing to move into wealth in your life?

_____
_____
_____
_____

2. What is the purpose of the sowing/reaping principle?

_____
_____

3. Using the priorities of a Christian listed at the end of the chapter, examine your life and write the order you put them in your own life.

_____
_____
_____
_____

# Chapter 2
Multiplying Money into Wealth

# Achieving Authentic Wealth

1. How is wealth achieved in your life?
   _____
   _____

2. What qualities can you cultivate in your life to qualify you for wealth?
   _____
   _____

3. What was Christ communicating when he was asked about the greatest commandment?
   _____
   _____
   _____

4. How have Christians in the western world abdicated their Christianity to others?
   _____
   _____
   _____

5. Going to church doesn't make you _____ any more than going into the ocean makes you a fish.

6. What can make Christianity a fruitless religion?
   _____
   _____

7. What separates supernatural success from prosperity?
   _____
   _____

# Chapter 2
## Multiplying Money into Wealth

8. To serve God is to do everything you do with _____ in mind.

9. The more time we spend with God, the more _____.

10. You become a more usable vessel for God's purposes through an _____ _____.

11. What is the heartbeat of God?
_____

12. The whole Bible is about God attempting to _____.

# Chapter 2
## Multiplying Money into Wealth

# Key Point Review

1. _____ does not make you faithful, nor is the accumulation of stuff a sign of God's _____ on your life.

2. Are there any ways you have abdicated your responsibilities to other Christians? How can you change that?

   _____
   _____
   _____
   _____

3. To serve God is to do everything you do with _____.

4. How can you foster change in your own life?

   _____
   _____

# Chapter 3
## How to Lose Your Wealth

# Achieving Authentic Wealth

1. What does God desire of you above your personal prosperity?
   _____

2. What does God desire to do with those things that could hinder our relationship with Him?
   _____
   _____

3. God desires the _____ and the _____ of our life to be in Him.

4. Why is inward obedience so important?
   _____
   _____
   _____

5. What is the greatest threat to our God-given wealth and prosperity?
   _____
   _____

6. What does it mean to worship? What is the object of worship in a person's life?
   _____
   _____
   _____

7. What happens when we try to frame the Word around our self-purposes and experiences?
   _____
   _____

# Chapter 3
## How to Lose Your Wealth

8. What is the greatest hindrance in the church that prevents it fom fulfilling the Great Commission?

_____
_____


9. What problems does a ministry, church, or individual have that are constantly in need of money?

_____
_____


10. What is a storehouse?

_____
_____


11. What does the scripture say about destroying our wealth?

_____
_____

# Chapter 3
## How to Lose Your Wealth

# Key Point Review

1. The greatest threat to our God-given prosperity is _____.


2. _____ keeps Christians and churches from being able to give to support the advancement of the Gospel.


3. More money will come when we have been proven faithful with _____ and _____ with what we have.

# Chapter 4
## Creating Generational Wealth

**Achieving Authentic Wealth**

1. What is an inheritance?
   _____
   _____

2. To hide something is to _____.

3. Why do animals store food?
   _____
   _____

4. How can we apply that concept to the wealth in our lives?
   _____
   _____
   _____

5. What does knowing the Word of God help us do?
   _____
   _____

6. What is accomplished with meditating on the Word?
   _____
   _____
   _____

7. Knowledge is really of no great benefit to you unless you have _____.

# Chapter 4
## Creating Generational Wealth

8. How can you make your faith grow?

9. How does our inner change manifest itself in our lives?

10. What is _____ is what is believed; what is _____ is what becomes evident in your life.

11. What four things are included in the act of confession?

12. How can meditation on evil be detrimental?

13. Whose responsibility is it to disciple children?

14. What four things should you do to disciple your children?

___

15. Why did the generations after Joshua fall into idolatry?

___

16. What is a gate?

___

17. What is the greatest respect, admiration, and love a person can give to another?

___

# Chapter 4
# Creating Generational Wealth

# Chapter 4
## Creating Generational Wealth

# Key Point Review

1. What is a great man?

   _____

   _____


2. Knowing the Word of God instantly helps us to _____ and _____ vain imaginations and the darts our enemy would try to confuse us with.


3. The inward change manifests itself outwardly through our responses to the _____ and _____ of life.


4. What is confession?

   _____

   _____


5. Teaching kids also makes you _____ to them for your own relationship with them.

# Chapter 5
## How to Maintain the Wealth and Blessing of God

# Achieving Authentic Wealth

1. What determines the end result when two people are in the same place with the same opportunity?

   _____
   _____
   _____
   _____

2. What causes God to make provision for our future success?

   _____
   _____

3. What happens when someone fails to repent or admit fault?

   _____
   _____
   _____

4. What is a legalistic mentality?

   _____
   _____

5. We have always had the mindset that God's commands are about what we _____ as opposed to what we _____.

6. Why is only having the "necessities" not enough?

   _____
   _____
   _____

# Chapter 5
## How to Maintain the Wealth and Blessing of God

7. _____ is personal and indicates that it changes with time.

8. What does it mean to "love the Lord your God"?
   _____
   _____
   _____

9. Why is it important to be able to see God and His steps?
   _____
   _____

**Chapter 5**
**How to Maintain the Wealth and Blessing of God**

# Key Point Review

1. God's commands are given for our _____ and to prevent us from _____.

2. Having only the _____ cannot bless others. They can only meet _____.

3. Love does not _____, it _____.

4. _____ and _____ have a far greater purpose and plan than what I can get from them for my personal consumption.

# Chapter 6
## The Real Purpose of Wealth

# Achieving Authentic Wealth

1. What does the term occupy mean?

2. Who will drive out the nations of the earth? What does that mean?

3. What is God's ultimate purpose and plan on the earth?

4. What admission did Christ make in Matthew 9 regarding the harvest?

5. Why is financial wealth given to us?

6. What happens when we spend our wealth on self-consumption?

# Chapter 6
# The Real Purpose of Wealth

7. What is it that occupies and dispossesses the nations?
___
___
___

8. We can never limit what needs to be done by _____.
We must look beyond our own _____, our own current _____,
and even our own _____.

9. If we are to dispossess nations, we have to _____.

10. Persistence plus time equals _____.

11. What happens after we go to the city or nation that God has set aside for us to occupy with the gospel?
___
___

12. What happens when we idly choose to ignore God's plan?
___
___

13. What happens with God's purpose and plan when we spend it on our own consumption?
___
___

# Chapter 6
## The Real Purpose of Wealth

# Key Point Review

1. We must look beyond our own _____, our own current _____, and our own _____.

2. What things do you feel that God is pushing you to do in your life with regard to His ultimate plan?

_____
_____
_____
_____

3. In what ways could you possibly be limiting these plans?

_____
_____
_____
_____

4. What must you do to put yourself in a position to see God begin to bring the victory for you to accomplish His will?

_____
_____
_____
_____

# Chapter 7
Blessing or Curse, It's Your Choice

1. A _____ usually consists of more than one option for making a _____.

2. God may put a vision in your heart for the future, but what He requires is that today _____.

3. How can we make good decisions?
   _____
   _____

4. What is the Holy Spirit consistent in with regard to making choices?
   _____
   _____

5. Is it God's responsibility to bless what we decide to do? What choice must we make?
   _____
   _____

6. What must happen for curses to be reversed?
   _____
   _____

7. What happens when you depend on others for your needs rather than God?
   _____
   _____

8. Cursed does not always mean _____. It means nothing will be _____.

# Chapter 7
## Blessing or Curse, It's Your Choice

9. If you find yourself without enough money, you may not have an _____ problem; you may have a _____ problem.

10. If God says He will give instruction, it is our responsibility to _____ it. We must put ourselves in the position to see and know _____.

11. The _____ of God is about having a vision for others, while the _____ of God is consuming God's favor on yourself.

12. What does disobedience do in our walk with God?
_____
_____

13. _____ is not the mandate of God. The _____ of unbelievers and the _____ of Jesus are His commands.

14. What gods are we choosing to follow when we disobey God?
_____
_____

# Chapter 7
## Blessing or Curse, It's Your Choice

# Key Point Review

1. In your own words, what does Deuteronomy 11:26-28 communicate?

_____
_____
_____
_____

2. What things should you allow for to make a good decision?

_____
_____
_____
_____

3. _____ does not always mean something will be taken away, it means that nothing will be _____.

4. We bring harm to ourselves and curse ourselves because of a choice to _____.

# Chapter 8
Consider Abraham

# Achieving Authentic Wealth

1. What do you usually do when you consider something?
   _____
   _____

2. What was the New Testament established with?
   _____
   _____

3. The covenant through Jesus Christ did not do away with the covenant given to Abraham - _____.

4. According to Christ, how do we know if we are children of Abraham?
   _____
   _____

5. What mentality did the Jews have concerning their righteousness and how did it compare with Abraham's righteousness?
   _____
   _____
   _____
   _____

6. Abraham did not start out in life a _____.

7. Everywhere Abraham went, everywhere he stopped had a _____.

8. How many landmarks did Abraham pass by between Genesis 11:31 and Genesis 13:4?
   _____

# Chapter 8
# Consider Abraham

9. What are some insights we can gather from verses between Genesis 11:31 and Genesis 13:4?

_____
_____
_____
_____
_____
_____
_____
_____

10. What are some additional thoughts within the context of the story of Abraham that we can gather?

_____
_____
_____
_____
_____
_____

# Chapter 8
**Consider Abraham**

# Key Point Review

1. Everywhere Abraham stopped had a _____.

2. _____ will always be the one constant in the pursuit of success.

3. You will be tested under trial to give back to God the very thing He _____ _____.

4. Looking at your life, what significant stops have you had to make on the journey and how did they benefit you?

_____
_____
_____
_____
_____
_____

# Chapter 9
Leave... And Go to the Land I Will Show You

# Achieving Authentic Wealth

1. So many times we Christians receive the _____ and understand the _____ to which God has called us.

2. What situations have you been faced with where you have felt you should bypass the things that stand between you and God's destination for you? What was the result of trying to bypass these things?

_____
_____
_____
_____
_____
_____

3. Where does our focus tend to shift when we receive a promise from God?

_____
_____

4. What will stop us from seeing the fulfillment of God's promises in our lives?

_____
_____

5. What takes priority over everything else in our lives?

_____
_____

6. What happens if our life is not tempered by the character of Christ?

_____
_____

7. What must happen with our dreams and promises that God has given to us before they will succeed?

_____
_____

Chapter 9
Leave... And Go to the Land I Will Show You

# Chapter 9
## Leave... And Go to the Land I Will Show You

# Key Point Review

1. Something in us believes we should _____ the things that stand between us and where God wants us to be.

2. Why is it important to go through the things that are between us and our destination?
   _____
   _____

3. Why does God want to temper our dreams and promises?
   _____
   _____

# Chapter 10
Leave Ur

## Achieving Authentic Wealth

1. What was the city of Ur in the days of Abraham?
   _____
   _____

2. How could one paraphrase the verses in Genesis where Abraham was commanded to leave Ur?
   _____
   _____
   _____
   _____

3. In the new Testament, what would this command be equated to?
   _____

4. Salvation is not just being saved from something; it is _____
   _____.

5. Why can we not be almost committed to God?
   _____
   _____

6. What does the literal meaning of the word Ur mean?
   _____

7. God has made _____ for your escape.

# Chapter 10
## Leave Ur

# Chapter 10
## Leave Ur

# Key Point Review

1. What was Abraham required to leave when he was commanded to leave Ur?

_____

_____

_____


2. What is salvation for?

_____

_____


3. If you stay in this place called Ur and do not repent and leave your worldly lifestyle to pursue Christ with all your energy, you will _____.

# Chapter 11
## They Came to Haran

1. Where was the city of Haran located?

2. What can we not assume has happened when we leave Ur? How was this demonstrated in Abraham's life?

3. What is one reason we do not fulfill our purpose in life?

4. What do Christians today believe to be true because they are blessed? What is the truth in this matter?

# Chapter 11
## They Came to Haran

**Chapter 11**
**They Came to Haran**

# Key Point Review

1. How can you tell when you have truly left Ur?

2. How was Abraham still not considered a blessing when he left Ur?

3. In what ways could you be delaying your fulfillment of God's purpose in your life?

# Chapter 12
## He Set Out from Haran

# Achieving Authentic Wealth

1. Where is "The tree of Moreh" derived from and what does it mean?
   _____
   _____
   _____

2. At what times in our lives are we sometimes stopped for sound biblical and doctrinal truth to be established?
   _____
   _____
   _____

3. Why do churches fail to teach foundational, doctrinal truth?
   _____
   _____

4. How is the responsibility for our growth often put on church leadership?
   _____
   _____
   _____

5. Why do most people fail to educate and discipline themselves?
   _____
   _____
   _____

6. The real place of the revelation of Christ is in _____.

# Chapter 12
## He Set Out from Haran

7. What should our attitude be toward the "hidden" word of God?

   _____

   _____

8. How long should someone stay in a place before moving on to the next area of life?

   _____

   _____

9. What does the word "Shechem" mean? What is the purpose of this place?

   _____

   _____

   _____

# Chapter 12
## He Set Out from Haran

# Key Point Review

1. Moreh is the place where we can gain _____, _____, and an _____ to hopefully use in our future.

2. We cannot enact _____ in the Word if we do not _____ it.

3. The place of _____ should always prepare us for the next journey to the next _____ or stop that God has for us.

# Chapter 13
## He Went On Toward the Hills

# Achieving Authentic Wealth

1. What did the original name for Bethel (Luz) mean?
   _____
   _____

2. What does the name "Bethel" mean?
   _____
   _____

3. What does the name "Ai" mean?
   _____
   _____

4. What can we deduct from what the scripture tells us about where Abraham pitched his tent?
   _____
   _____

5. What two results can your time in Ai cause to happen in your life?
   _____
   _____
   _____
   _____

6. Bethel, or the house of God, could be illustrated as the _____.

7. A house is where someone _____, their _____.

# Chapter 13
## He Went On Toward the Hills

8. The house of God represents the place God _____ or _____.

9. Based on this example, what two meanings can we understand?
   _____
   _____

10. If we ever hope to survive and move on from Ai, we must _____
    _____.

11. Why should you not depend on the church for your intimacy and experience with God?
    _____
    _____
    _____

# Chapter 13
## He Went On Toward the Hills

# Key Point Review

1. Bethel can be translated to mean _____.

2. In all of our lives we will experience _____ and _____.

3. We can visit and dwell under the _____ of God's Holy Spirit through and during times of worship.

4. Should you depend on the church for your intimacy with God? Why?
_____
_____
_____
_____

# Chapter 14
Set Out and Continue

# Achieving Authentic Wealth

1. What does the word "Negev" mean?
   _____
   _____

2. You must realize that avoiding Negev or detouring around it _____
   _____.

3. The Negev is about _____.

4. When you look at the life of Abraham, what places did he leave and where did he go?
   _____
   _____
   _____

5. What do we usually do when we reach our own personal "Negev"?
   _____
   _____
   _____

6. The Great Commission was never supposed to be in the _____.

7. What two results can the Negev have on an individual?
   _____
   _____

# Chapter 14
## Set Out and Continue

8. What four things can we do to ensure our success in the Negev?

_____

_____

_____


9. _____ follows _____, suggesting that what we learn in "Moreh" needs to be put into practice in "_____."


10. What is our mandate?

_____

_____


11. God desires our _____ with a purpose.


12. Our personal wealth and prosperity can be submitted to the _____ of the Holy Spirit.


13. What must happen if you want to be anything supernatural or extraordinary?

_____

_____

# Chapter 14
**Set Out and Continue**

# Key Point Review

1. Is the desert meant only for those who are disobedient? Why?

   _____
   _____
   _____

2. God sends light into _____ places, and salt to places that _____.

3. What would and could God trust us with if we had the ability to always do what He _____ _____ when He _____.

4. What is temperance?

   _____
   _____
   _____
   _____

# Chapter 15
Went Down to Egypt

# Achieving Authentic Wealth

1. What does the term "copula" mean?
   _____
   _____

2. During what times in life are we forced to leave a place God brought us to?
   _____
   _____

3. What two things can happen when we make a wrong decision at a wrong time?
   _____
   _____
   _____
   _____
   _____

4. Why do some Christians never grow?
   _____
   _____

5. What happens if you prematurely leave a stop or stage in your life?
   _____
   _____

6. What is the first thing Abraham did while he was in Egypt?
   _____
   _____

# Chapter 15
## Went Down to Egypt

7. What can easily set us on our way to financial success?

8. What kind of people should we spend our time with?

9. What is the greatest form of gratitude we can show to people from whom we want to learn?

10. What is the second thing Abraham did while in Egypt?

11. God blesses the hands of the _____.

12. What kind of person does God withhold financial blessing from?

13. What does the word "acquire" mean?

14. What must you do before you can see personal blessing in your own life?

15. What is the greatest asset you will ever possess to make money?

16. What is the greatest liability you will ever possess to lose money?

17. What is the third thing Abraham did while he was in Egypt?

18. What are the two most important words any vibrant Christian should know, understand, and practice?

19. What will living in and being surrounded by a worldly system require you to do?

# Chapter 15
## Went Down to Egypt

# Chapter 15
## Went Down to Egypt

# Key Point Review

1. Just because something is causing you to _____ and _____ _____ does not give you spiritual affirmation to pick up and leave.

2. _____ to stay where you are is the biggest reason we do not change.

3. God's favor can be upon us to connect us to the _____ at the _____.

4. Whose hands does God bless?
_____
_____

5. Whose hands will God not bless?
_____
_____

6. Why should you benefit your employer?
_____
_____
_____

7. Being in the world, one of two things will happen - it will _____, or you will _____.

# Chapter 16
## He Went from Place to Place

**Achieving Authentic Wealth**

1. What could make a person think they are exempt from the sanctifying process of God?
   _____
   _____

2. Why did God create wealth for men?
   _____

3. What does being tempered in the Negev with our wealth do for us?
   _____
   _____
   _____

4. What did the Bible mean when it said that Abraham moved from place to place?
   _____
   _____

5. Why does God not always tell us where to go and what to do?
   _____
   _____

6. Keep moving until you discover _____.

7. Does obedience to God mean always making the perfect decision every time? Why?
   _____
   _____

# Chapter 16
## He Went from Place to Place

8.  What course of action will require us to "miss God"?
    _____
    _____

# Chapter 16
## He Went from Place to Place

# Key Point Review

1. In what way can wealth and God's blessing be a hindrance to you?

2. Why does God not always tell us where to go?

3. What actions are considered by critics to be "missing God's will"?

4. What actions will really make a person "miss God's will"?

# Chapter 17
## He Came to Bethel

# Achieving Authentic Wealth

1. What is the local and universal church's purpose?
   _____
   _____

2. What are the purposes that the church should be overseeing?
   _____
   _____

3. What is the biggest reason most churches split? What are usually the issues involved?
   _____
   _____
   _____

4. To not exercise _____ is to walk in _____.

5. What did Abraham prove was possible regarding ministry and business people?
   _____
   _____

6. What is the role of the minister, as Melchizedek demonstrated with Abraham?
   _____
   _____

7. What does the ministry exist for? What is our role as a congregation?
   _____
   _____

# Chapter 17
## He Came to Bethel

8. What would need to happen for the Great Commission to be completed in a generation?

_____

_____

_____

_____

9. How are we influenced by the company we keep?

_____

_____

_____

# Chapter 17
## He Came to Bethel

# Key Point Review

1. The church's purpose is to _____ and carry out the _____ and _____ of God.

2. Why do pastors with a vision usually lack to see that vision come to pass?
   _____

3. The church needs _____ - _____ are the church. The church needs _____ to do what God has commissioned it to do.

4. Just because we have enjoyed _____, _____, and _____ does not mean our life is complete.

# Chapter 18
Lot Was Moving About with Abram

# Achieving Authentic Wealth

1. Who was with Abraham in Genesis 13:5-13? What observations can be made about this individual?

   _____
   _____

2. What four things can be observed from Abraham's confrontation with his nephew?

   _____
   _____
   _____
   _____

3. What does the name "Sodom" mean?

   _____

4. What does the name "Gomorrah" mean?

   _____

5. What does the name "Zoar" mean? Why did Lot escape to this place?

   _____
   _____

6. Based on the definition of "Zoar," what life did Lot have to look forward to there?

   _____
   _____

# Chapter 18
## Lot Was Moving About with Abram

**Chapter 18**
**Lot Was Moving About with Abram**

# Key Point Review

1. Why did Lot make the wrong choice of where to settle?
   _____
   _____

2. Lot, having had everything, had to live out his days in the place of _____. No _____, no _____, only surviving.

3. What is life and service to God about?
   _____
   _____

4. What is life and service to God not about?
   _____
   _____

# Chapter 19
The Lord Said to Abram

1. Why would Abraham have not made it as far without going through all he had been through?

2. When faced with the choice of following God's plan or our own undisciplined way, what characteristics usually determine how successful we will be?

3. What meanings does the word "Hebron" have? What do the words mean when put together?

4. Because of his experience with God, what has Abraham become?

5. What qualified Abraham to be the steward and distributor of God's blessing?

6. What two things did Abraham possess that he could redistribute to the world?

# Chapter 19
## The Lord Said to Abram

# Chapter 19
# The Lord Said to Abram

# Key Point Review

1. In your own life, what experiences have you been through that have been essential to getting you where you are? How do they compare with Abraham's experience?

_____

_____

_____

_____

_____

_____

2. Abraham was to establish the _____, the _____, and the _____ through the blessing of God in the whole earth.

3. Life that we see through Jesus' example to us is about _____.

# Chapter 20
The Purpose of Prosperity

**Achieving Authentic Wealth**

1. Poverty is an insult to the _____ of persons.

2. What constitutes true prosperity or true success?
   _____
   _____
   _____

3. _____ is often a mocking deceiver.

4. Do we have moral responsibility to the poor? Why?
   _____
   _____
   _____

5. Giving to God always produces _____.

6. What are "financial counselors" misleading people to believe?
   _____
   _____

7. What happens when we give? How are we releasing it in faith?
   _____
   _____
   _____

8. Who was Jesus born to? How is this important in regards to His ministry?
   _____
   _____

# Chapter 20
## The Purpose of Prosperity

9. What could one write as the thesis statement of this book?

10. What are the six simple, basic thoughts that are reviewed in this chapter?

# Chapter 20
## The Purpose of Prosperity

# Key Point Review

1. How is poverty an insult?

2. What are the different definitions of prosperity that are held by different people?

3. What is meant by the statement "You Can't Take It With You"?

4. In what ways can you minister to the poor as Christ did?

5. How have you personally observed the six basic thoughts outlined in the chapter in your own life?

# Resources of Interest

**Character is King**
*Dr. John Binkley*

*It's a Guy Thing: Character is King* takes you on your dream journey. There is a place called destiny that we all journey to. We all have ideas, dreams and vision for what life should be. This book lays out a plan for that journey to realizing your dreams, and to your destiny.

**Let's Talk About Sex**
*Dr. John A. King*

Let's face it. Sexuality is all around us. It's even on billboards, magazines and television commercials. Sadly, It's a topic many men and women have to deal with on their own because too many churches or pastors won't touch it. Find out what the Bible has to say about some of the toughest questions in *Let's Talk About Sex*.

**Now to Next**
*Dr. John A. King*

What does the next generation church look like? Who are the people that will be involved in the next generation church? How will it come about?

Those are some of the questions answered in Dr. King's newest release, *Now to Next: Blueprint for a Christian Revolution*.

**Helping Guys Become Men, Husbands, and Fathers**
*Dr. John A. King*

*It's a Guy Thing* takes you on the journey of fatherhood. Dr. John King shares the skills necessary to become a good father. He shows you what can happen when a father is absent or simply not active in a child's life. Being a male is a matter of birth. Being a man is a matter of choice. This book will help you make that choice.

To see all the titles available through Guy Thing Press, visit us online at www.guythingpress.com

# Resources of Interest

**Business By The Book**
*Dr. John A. King*

The world's greatest handbook on leadership, economic and social excellence is not found in schoolbooks, but in Scripture. The principles in this book are tried, proven and resilient over centuries. Christ bet His life on it, and so can you.

**Show Me the Money**
*Dr. John A. King*

Time Magazine asked, "Does God want you to be rich?" The answer to that question is simply "No, God wants you to be *wealthy*." In *Show Me the Money*, you will learn the fundamentals of creating and using wealth in God's kingdom.

**Achieving Authentic Wealth**
*Jeff McLoud*

We need a vision that goes beyond our ability to be consumers only. A vision so big, so powerful, that we cannot even accomplish it in our own lifetime - a vision founded from the very heartbeat of God. We could see the vision fulfilled if we ask ourselves a simple question: "How can we achieve twice as much with half the money?"

**Creating a Better Life**
*Erik A. Kudlis*

In this easy to read manual, educator and administrator turned international businessman, Erik Kudlis, identifies three vital keys you must know and use, given by God Himself, that unlock the doors to the life God has always wanted you to have.

To see all the titles available through Guy Thing Press, visit us online at www.guythingpress.com

# Further Resources

### The Godly Man Curriculum

The Godly Man Curriculum is designed to train men from all walks of life, giving them a firm foundation of doctrine and Godly knowledge. This curriculum is available both over the internet for individual study and on DVD for seminars, Sunday schools, and men's meetings. With up to 7 hours of video teaching divided over numerous topics, the Godly Man Curriculum is an excellent tool that you can build your classes upon and grow yourself and your people.

Listen to sample teachings from the Godly Man Curriculum at www.imnonline.org.

### Building Iron Men & Life As Leaders Networks

The Building Iron Men and Life as Leaders networks are two of IMN's finest resources. Each network provides you with a new teaching every month that will challenge and encourage you to grow. The Building Iron Men network features three teachings in both CD and DVD format that are tailored for men, while the Life as Leaders network provides you with three CDs that teach leadership principles anyone can use.

Both networks are phenomenal tools that are vital assets to any church and discipleship program.

## Also check out these websites for great resources and training materials.

International Men's Network
www.imnonline.org

Guy Thing Press
www.guythingpress.com

The International Men's Network was founded by Dr. John A. King. Its purpose is to help men grow to become the leaders their families and churches need and become men of God that make a lasting impact on those around them.

IMN is a missionary organization to the men of the world. We are committed to:

- Inspire all men to rise to a high standard of biblical manhood.
- Encourage them to excel in their roles as men, leaders, husbands, and fathers.
- Challenge them to be contributors to society and set an example based upon a biblical value system that will benefit this generation and lay a solid foundation for the next generation.

The International Men's Network is dedicated to providing and hosting the best resources for men, including teachings and lessons on CD and DVD and conferences that teach men the principles that will help them become more influential and effective in their lives.

For more information about IMN and its mission, visit us online at www.imnonline.org or call 817.993.0047

The Christian Life Center was founded by Dr. John King and his wife, Beccy. With a vision to preach the gospel of Jesus Christ with unashamed passion and uncompromising truth, Christian Life Center aims to raise up the next generation of leaders to move into all the world and proclaim the truth of Christ to the lost and broken.

Located in the Keller, Texas area, the church sits in the prime location to reach the community and the people therein. The church desires to give back to the community by providing outreaches to better and enrich its inhabitants. From kickboxing classes that are aimed at teaching children and adults self-defense, to a special service that commemorates and honors our country's war-time heroes, Christian Life Center strives to bring a living Jesus to a dying world by new and imaginative means that will bless and change lives.

For more information about Christian Life Center and the resources it offers, visit the website at www.clctx.org